Google Classroom

How to Benefit from Distance Learning and Setup Your Virtual Classroom.

Arthur Tyrrell

Contents

Introduction

In the past, education was provided in the gurukul – students (formerly called shishya) used to be taught about the various aspects of life under trees by a single guru (teacher). With the coming of modernization, this was not the case as humanity started building establishments for education and learning – a place where people came together to gain instruction on different subjects.

Technology in these times has turned out to be an essential constituent of our society; we see it employed in the production processes, entertainment, finance, and now even in education. In fact, technology is now seen as a tool that can be used to reach children who have no actual access to schools and, as such, cannot get an education. With the advancements in technology, social interaction has become easy, and that has, in turn, branched to make communication between educators and pupils quite easy. Nowadays, students do not need to go to traditional classrooms to get an education as technology has provided an avenue for smart/digital education – a teacher can be in one location and teach students who are in a different place via the internet or web. Further advancement in technology has got the world experiencing what we now know as "Smart classrooms" and "Smart software."

Smart software has gone a long way to change the direction of our educational system. It is organized in a fashion such that what the students' needs are put into consideration, and groundbreaking learning methods of teaching with the aid of digital instructional materials such as projectors, whiteboards, online apps, and use of smartphones are employed. Furthermore, smart software goes on to help in school management in the sense that it provides automatic software to handle database information, thus leaving out more than enough time to focus on the actual objectives of education, which is to provide instruction to students. In this, smart software is a program that aims to transform the approach and methods employed in modern education.

Chapter 1

Google Classroom

Google Classroom is a gratuitous service that is available on the internet, created by Google for institutions of education. What Google Classroom aims to make the development, distribution, and grading of assignments easy and in a way that does not involve the utilization of paper. So overall, the underlying objective of Google Classroom is to create a direct link for which files can be shared between students and their teachers.

Google Classroom has a couple of Google apps that are integrated with it to make the sharing of files betwixt instructors and their students possible. For example, an instructor teacher can use Google Drive to create assignments as well as distribute the tasks to his/her students. Google Docs, Google Sheets, and Google Slides can be used to write. Gmail provides a platform for the files to be shared, as well as for further information to be passed across. Lastly, Google Calendar can be used to schedule the time and date where the assignments can be submitted.

Furthermore, a teacher can invite his/her students to join a class via a private code, or an invitation can be sent to them from the school domain. Every class is separate and will be treated like that in the Google Classroom; a separate folder will be created for each class in the Drive of each user (student or teacher), and that way, students can submit their completed assignments to their teacher for grading.

Apps in mobile phones, Android, or iOS, allow the students to take pictures and have them attached to assignments, transfer files using other apps, and get access to some additional information offline. Teachers are also equipped to keep tabs on the progress of their students from the submitted assignments. Once they are done scoring and grading the assignments, they can return them to the students, alongside appropriate comments.

Google Classroom brings about more productivity in teaching and learning in the following ways: assignments are streamlined, increased collaboration, and advocating communication between students and teachers. Teachers or instructors can create classes, allocate assignments, send feedback to their students, and more in one place. Moreover, schools and nonprofit organizations can get Google Classroom for free since it is a core service available under G Suite for Education and G Suite for Nonprofits, it is also a service available under G Suite for Enterprise and G Suite for Business.

Smart learning

Digital/smart education system is a kind of educational system that employs the use of a wide range of digital tools such as smartphones, tablets, laptops, projectors, starboards, digital textbooks, and more for teaching and learning purposes. Students are taught using audio-visual learning tools, and the teacher must guide the students through the courses in a fashion that is tailored to the learning pace of the student (progress is determined by how much of the subject matter the student can grasp).

Digital learning classrooms do not require the physical attendance of the students, as is the case with the traditional method of learning; rather, in digital/smart learning, students take their courses/classes online.

History

Google Classroom was first announced on the 6th of May 2014, and a preview was shown to a couple of members of the G Suite for Education program, and it wasn't until the 12th of August that same year that it was released to the public. The following year, Google announced a Classroom Application Programming Interface (API) and a share button for websites in a bid to enable administrators of various schools as well as developers to connect with Google Classroom. Again in 2015, Google integrated Google Calendar into Google Classroom so that teachers can schedule the due dates for assignments they give to their students, dates for field trips, and class speakers.

In 2017, Google Classroom was opened to the general public, permitting any personal Google user to join classes without having to own a G Suite for Education account (up until then, the G Suite for Education account was required), and in April 2017, Google made it possible for personal users of Google to create and teach a class.

In 2018, Google made the following announcements; an addition of a classroom refresh, addition of classwork section, improved grading interface, permitting reuse of school assignment from classes that have been taken before, and addition of features that will enable teachers to organize their content based on the topic.

In 2019, Google added 78 new pictorial themes and created an option for users to drag and drop topics as well as schoolwork in the classwork section.

Features

Google Classroom combines Google Drive, Google Docs, Google Sheets, Google Slides, and Gmail altogether to aid institutions of education to enter an era where the paper isn't required to get schoolwork done. Google Calendar was incorporated into the Classroom a little later to aid in assignment due dates, field trips, and class speakers. The database of students in any institution can be put into Google Classroom, and through the database, students can be invited to join using a private code which will be added to the user interface of the student later, or, it could be transferred from the domain of the school automatically. A new folder is created in the Google Drive of any every user whenever a new class is created with Google Classroom, and from that folder, students can submit their assignments and projects to their teachers.

Assignments

Assignments and projects that students submit are marked and stacked away on Google's suite of productivity applications. It is this suite that creates an avenue for cooperation between instructors and pupils or amongst students. Because of this, a student is not required to share documents that are on his/her Google Drive with their teacher; instead, the assignments and projects are hosted on the Drive of the student, and then they are submitted for grading. A teacher could select a file which they have determined to be used as an outline, and from this outline, each student is to edit and make their changes to the document, which they can then submit for grading. Students in need of more grades are even allowed to attach certain related documents from their Drive to the assignment.

Grading

There are various forms of grading systems that are supported by Google Classroom. If a teacher wants to, he/she can attach certain files to the assignments they create so students can view, edit, or acquire a copy of the files for themselves. On the other hand, students are also permitted to create their own files and have them attached to their assignments if their teacher didn't create any files. More so, teachers can supervise the progress their students are making from the assignments submitted by the students, and they can even edit and add comments. Once students submit their assignments and/or project reports, the teacher grades them and returns them to the students with comments and suggestions on how they can do better if they did something wrong; on getting the assignment, the student can then review and make corrections where necessary after which they submit the assignment again. Note that assignments must be marked by a teacher; only then can the assignment be edited; students can only edit their assignments when their teachers return the assignments to them.

Communication

In the Classroom, a teacher can post an announcement to their class stream, and students can, in turn, comment on those announcements. Students are also allowed to post certain kinds of information to the class stream; however, it won't be treated with as high a priority as an announcement by a teacher, and the number of posts each student can make is subject to some kind of control – that is, they cannot make past a definite number of posts. Google Classroom supports the attachment of many types of media from the products that Google offers, and that includes videos from YouTube and files from Google Drive to announcements and posts, allowing for the sharing of content. One other service offered by Google, which is integrated into Google Classroom, is Gmail. Gmail enables teachers to send emails to one or more of their students via the Google Classroom platform. Access to the Google Classroom can be done on the internet or via mobile apps provided on either iOS or Android devices.

Originality Report

Earlier this year (January 2020), the originality report was introduced into the Google Classroom. The originality report makes it possible for teachers and students to view parts of the work they submit that contain the particular words or phrases that have been used by another author, this is to help curtail the incidence of plagiarism. For students, especially, the originality report brings source materials to the foreground and brings to the attention of the students the areas that require citations thus, assisting them in developing and becoming better writers. Teachers, on their end, can use the originality report to check for students' originality (that is, to see if students adhere to moral standards in academics) in the assignments they turn in. In G Suite for Education (free), teachers can activate originality reports for not more than three (3) assignments. However, there are no such limitations for G Suite Enterprise for Education (paid).

Archive course

A teacher can create an archive of the courses they have taught by the end of a term or year in Google Classroom. As soon as a teacher archives a particular course, that course is removed from the homepage and transferred into the folder titled Archived Classes; this way, a teacher can properly arrange and organize their classes. On the other hand, students won't be able to touch a course once it has been archived, they can, view it but until it is returned to the homepage, they won't be able to make any changes.

Mobile applications

Google Classroom also allows for mobile devices (that is, iOS and Android) access, and this began in January 2015. Users of these mobile devices who are part of the Classroom can take photos and then attach the photos to their assignments, and they can also transfer files using other apps, and even access the Classroom offline.

Privacy

In comparison to the consumer services offered by Google, which depict advertisements in their interface, Google Classroom, which is a component of the G Suite for Education, it does not allow for any displays of advertisements in its interface for either students, faculty, or teachers. Furthermore, user data is not scanned for the purpose of advertising or any such endeavors.

Reception

Google Classroom has been tested by the *eLearning Industry*, and they released a review showing some of the pros and cons that they observed. Some of the positive aspects of Google Classroom include; ease of usage, you can access it from any kind of device, teachers can easily and promptly share assignments with their students as the incorporation of Google Drive has proved to be very effective, paperless exchange of assignments and project reports which has brought printing, handing out, and potential loss of work to a stop, and finally, students can quickly get their assignments as soon as the teacher is done scoring and grading. But the negative aspects that were pointed out in the review are as follows; too much of Google apps and services were integrated into the Classroom, allowing little or no space for external services or files, there were no automatic quizzes or tests set up within the Classroom, there is no provision for live chat which would have proved helpful for feedback.

Criticism

Generally, Google's integrity has been questioned on many occasions, mostly because of issues that relate to privacy. Most of the criticisms placed on Google Classroom are no exception; people fear that the data they submit on the platform won't be protected. Sometimes, the criticism of Google Classroom is treated in a like manner as the criticism of Chromebooks and G Suite.

Furthermore, Google Classroom has been criticized because there is no properly designed grade book, automatic quizzes and tests which are a common attribute of learning management systems are lacking, and the ability to be able to edit an assignment after it has been released.

However, in response to the issues of worry relating to privacy, Google had this to say:

"Google is committed to building products that aid in protecting students as well as the teacher's privacy and provide best-in-class security for your institution."

Chapter 2
*Smart Education VS Traditional
Education System – Advantages and
Disadvantages*

Advantages

Flexibility

In the traditional system of education, students usually feel as though they have to meet up to their peers, especially when their peers are performing better in grasping subject matter effectively and efficiently. In contrast, the smart education system has no such pressures, the range of courses are designed in a fashion which allows students to learn at their own pace, they can also review the topics as much as they like and can even ask their teachers questions when they are having trouble understanding something.

Furthermore, students are permitted to acquire knowledge at a location of their choice – any environment they have deemed comfortable for learning rather than having to sit in a traditional classroom where they can be easily distracted or a library that is filled with people. Learning online allows a student the option to create an environment for themselves where they feel is conducive enough for learning. As such, a student can choose to take their courses online while sitting in their preferred café or in even in their homes, and they can set it up as they like, they can even play a soft song in the setting and have coffee sitting on the table.

Lower Costs

In a traditional learning setting, there are certain kinds of fees that each student has to pay to even be permitted within the environment of the school and then allowed to go into their classrooms and partake in the topic of instruction that has been prepared for the day, make use of school resources like the laboratory and library. This is not the case with online learning – as long as the students have the required tools and software, they can even be given discounts on the courses they applied for.

Larger Variety of Courses

Unlike the traditional learning setting, smart learning or online schooling is not constrained in any way by either space or time. This is one major reason why teachers can offer their students a lot of courses which they wouldn't be able to if they were teaching students in a traditional classroom. As a result, a student who learns anything online is better off because they have access to many courses, and the best part about it is that they can even gain knowledge at their own convenient time and locations.

Channels of Communications with Teachers

Another great perk that comes with learning online is that it supplies a plausibility of students, communicating with their teachers through various means. Rather than waiting till the class ends, a student who is learning online can send his/her teacher a mail or reach the teacher via the chatting board on the platform-if they have some questions that need answering. Once a student has access to either teachers, experts, or student guides, their confidence in a subject matter is developed.

The kind of students who will benefit more from smart education systems are students who naturally are introverts and find it hard to ask questions in the classroom.

Collaboration with Peers and Virtual Study Groups

Students who are taking online courses can also have social interactions as there are platforms that support online study groups. Students are free to join these study groups and cooperate with other students like them in order to learn better and faster. One advantage is that their minds become open to broad and new ideas that relate to their courses and, this way, they come to an understanding of the latest trends in the courses they are interested in and receive updates on recent developments on those courses from their fellow students.

Disadvantages

Lack of Social Learning

The medium of social learning is interrupted in smart education systems. By social learning, we mean the learning procedure where students learn through physical interaction with their peers. In social learning, students learn to lean on each other for support, and they also learn patterns of behavior that will ultimately shape their character and teach them to respect themselves and others. Although students get to engage their colleagues in interaction in the smart learning setting, their interactions are not direct, and students will, in the long run, feel isolated.

Extracurricular activities

In the traditional system of education, there is provision for extracurricular activities which offers students an avenue to discover themselves and see the other amazing things they are capable of. Extracurricular activities do a good job of enhancing the self-confidence of students and as well as the development of their personalities. Smart learning, on its end, has no such provisions.

In summary, the youth of our generation are being equipped with various digital skills, and this is thanks to the number of opportunities that smart or online learning provides. Contemporary smart schools offer students a vast amount of smart learning systems that employ the use of visual methods as well as technology to deliver instruction more effectively and efficiently. This way, the procedure for learning is enhanced, and the abilities of the next generation of students are developed.

When students learn in this way, their minds retain and recollect what they learn for a long period. These days, the access that humanity has to technology has broadened the minds of learners, and this is because of the enormous amount of information that is obtainable. Most of the time, traditional methods of teaching and learning are viewed as boring, but with the invention of smart learning systems, learning has turned into an otherwise fun and thrilling enterprise.

The system of smart learning does a lot to prepare a student for a workspace in the future through the impartation of relevant skills.

Chapter 3

Comparison between smart/digital
learning and traditional education

An inquiry into which system of education will be better for learning and beneficial for all education stakeholders.

Learning Material

In the traditional system of education, books are the only forms of learning materials that teachers offer their students, however, in digital/smart learning, students are open to multiple materials that they can refer to concerning a particular subject matter without any form of constraints, these materials include e-books, PDF's, online links to websites that have content that relates to the course.

School Management

In the traditional system of education, records of the activities that relate to the school, such as fees, attendance, examinations, payroll, and registers are kept in record books, running a higher risk of getting lost. However, if these records are stored in a server created for the school, that is, the school has an Enterprise Resource Planning (ERP) software, technology takes charge, and it becomes the job of machines to keep records of the daily function and activities of the school. That way, records of activities are kept in a more secure environment where there is no risk of loss.

Smart Classes

Education in a traditional setting has teachers making use of blackboards or whiteboards alongside books when they want to explain the subject matter to their students. In most cases, the class building where these subjects are taught is not managed correctly or, in other words, disheveled. In smart or digital learning, knowledge is bestowed on students through presentations that are visual such as animations, through projections, and even virtual reality.

Costs Involved

When educational institutes do not employ the use of electronic gadgets and the opportunity provided by the internet, they don't necessarily have to spend much, however, just because you offer a low-cost education to students does not mean that you provide a quality education that will result in the increase of the academic and overall performance of the students. Smart learning on its end is quite expensive, and there is no disputing that. Be that as it may, it has demonstrated on countless occasions that it is of more benefit in teaching and learning. The use of audio-visual aids, stimulates the interest of students, making them more inclined to pay attention to the subject matter being taught by their teachers.

Communication

In the traditional system of education., students, their parents, and teachers can only interact with themselves when they are having a face-to-face conversation. In smart learning, that is not necessary as the ability to communicate between these parties is improved because of the advancements in technology. Furthermore, PTA gatherings are not entirely essential as social media networks and emails can allow parents and teachers to communicate from their homes. Other mediums through which parents, teachers, and students can interact include instant messages, phone calls, portal messages, and SMS.

Considering the benefits that are derived from smart learning as compared to the traditional system of delivering instruction, it makes more sense that the management of schools should subscribe to smart learning.

Merits of Smart Classes

1. Unlimited and untimely access to the Expansive World of Online Information

On the internet, a lot of information exists, which is readily available to students who want it. Scores of data that relate to various subjects have already been stored on the web, and a smart class can draw out most of those online materials for use in teaching and learning.

Smart classes are more appreciated by students who spend their free time trying to gain more knowledge that exceeds what is meant to be treated in the curriculum of their courses. Furthermore, online materials can satisfy students' curiosity and help them become more creative.

Teachers who have access to online educational materials from different articles that have been published on the web can take some of those materials and present them to their students in an attractive presentation. In this way, education does not deal with printed information only, and thus, teaching and learning have a form of excitement and fun attached to it that would not be found boring by students.

2. Digital Tools help students to understand subjects better

The use of blackboards and whiteboards are soon becoming a thing of the, past as the evolution of man has allowed teachers to impart knowledge upon their students using PowerPoint presentations, Word documents, audio sessions, and video screenings and images. As the very popular saying goes, "A picture is worth a thousand words!", students are better equipped to grasp knowledge when it is presented with audio-visual materials. Other digital tools like CDs, pen drives, and PDF files can be emailed to students, and this greatly eliminates the stress of having to copy notes while in a class on the part of the students, and can also help them to focus better on the subject matter during class.

3. Benefit for Absentees

If students are absent for a smart class, they can still catch up with what they missed in contrast to the traditional education system where missing a day of school means the student has no way of fully catching up. Still, the explanation given in class by their teachers cannot be given again. However, with smart/digital learning, if a student misses a class, they can access that class still because each class is usually uploaded on the internet. All the student must do is download the lectures that were uploaded on the web. Although to gain access, they would have to provide a user ID and password. This saves the student the inconvenience of putting in serious effort in obtaining a note when you miss a class as there are digital notes that you can always access.

4. Development of an Interactive Environment

Using digital tools in education creates somewhat of an interactive environment in learning. In a smart class, there is quite a considerable level of transparency between students and their faculties. Since learning is now connected to pictures, maps, images, and animated videos, students can connect properly with their faculties and be more inclined to share their thoughts and ideas through pictorial representations without feeling pressure.

5. The perfect option for students with different IQs

When you enter each class, you'll find a variety of students with varying mental faculties and capabilities – some students are able to grasp subject matter immediately, while others require continuous explanations. Smart classes can help bridge this gap between students; as students will be learning through different media platforms, advanced technology sets an interesting stage for both learners and teachers, and this brings about a different perspective to learning since quite a lot can happen as an aftermath of the visual outcomes of a smart class.

Therefore, smart classes present an environment for students to grasp subject matter either once or having to access the details of the subject more times for better understanding.

Demerits of Smart Classes

1. The problem of cost

Management of schools should endeavor to try to adopt the most modern forms of technology in their educational institutes. On a daily basis, new software is created, and it will be far from the truth to say that some of these new packages are not expensive, however, if you are to provide quality education to their wards under your supervision, school management ought to attempt to provide these resources that will do quite a lot to foster learning.

Another issue which might bring up a budgetary concern is having to train staff to use the recent technological gadgets and software, because the truth is not all members of staff are able to get used to making use of technologically-backed tools of learning.

2. Peril of Technology-Based Learning

The application of technology to educational processes yields productive and progressive results mostly because students tend to find the learning process entertaining. The one danger that comes with the continuous use of electronic gizmos is that students tend to depend too much on them in the long-run and that will hamper their ability to solve problems on their own, and this will be a serious especially if the electronic gadgets that a student is using begins to falter or misfunction. The parents of our generation are a little behind when we talk about incorporating technology in education, and most of them do not have the required knowledge or skills to use technology. This puts their children at a disadvantage since the parents are not able to assist their children with their assignments and projects.

3. Human Values

The teaching equipment required in a smart class is mainly electronic gizmos, and once students become used to learning via the use of digital devices, they will see no need to contact their teachers and, therefore, the relevance of their teachers will be lost on them which will indefinitely bring down the importance of really good teachers. Students will also become more attached to digital devices and look upon their teachers as nothing but a mere entity.

4. Monotonous Learning Process

Irrespective of the fact that smart classes bring a fun and exciting aspect to learning, too much reliance on the use of digital tools will bring down creative ability in a student. A class that is driven with technology tends to make the learning process look like more of a routine and a student's own brilliance, or intelligence tends to have reduced priority; the process of education becomes mechanical as students engage the use of digital devices that work in a certain way in a regular manner.

5. Technical probs

When an electronic device falters or misfunctions, a lot of teaching and learning hours become lost, and since these devices are most often than not, delicate; it requires a lot of time and cash to procure new ones or fix the broken ones. When that happens, teachers will have no choice but to go back to the blackboard or whiteboard mode of delivering instruction; this will undoubtedly be met with a lot of opposition from students, especially those who will not be willing to accept the alteration. As a result, the environment for learning will be suppressed, and this will be a burden to the teachers.

In Summary, smart classes have disadvantages, but if we are to compare these disadvantages with the disadvantages that come with traditional modes of education, we will find that the disadvantages of technology-backed education pale in comparison.

Chapter 4

Google Classroom and its Benefits

1. Simple-to-Use Tool

Google Classroom offers an exceptionally intuitive and excessively simple-to-learn interface. The platform talks you through each progression of the procedure. It is anything but difficult to utilize. "Google Classroom's build-up deliberately makes the instructional interface simple and options used for conveying and following-up assignments; correspondence with the whole course or people is additionally rearranged through announcements, email, and message pop-ups. At the point when you land on the main page of your classroom, you'll be welcome to "communicate with your class here." You can establish announcements and program them to go out on your own time. You can also respond to student notes. The interface is easy to grasp, which implies that there's no special learning or adaptation required to utilize the software. Google classroom is anything but difficult.

2. Class creation and student addition

Google Classroom permits you to create a one of a kind class for each class that you instruct. In only three mouse clicks and a couple of keystrokes, you can create a class. Google Classrooms are partitioned into various areas.

In the Students' area, you can see all the participants currently in your class. Students can be added manually, or they can join on their own utilizing their own Google account. At the point when you create a class, Google Classroom provides you with a class code located on the left-hand side of the screen. Share that class code with the students you want to join. From their PCs or Chromebooks, students sign into their Google files and utilize the class code to join.

Inside the Student segment, you can likewise decide whether your students are permitted to remark on the questions, announcements, and assignments you create or if they can just post at all. If you want, you can likewise decide to be the one in particular who can post and remark in your class.

In the stream area, you'll discover the assignments, announcements, and questions that you create. This area is where you'll invest the majority of your energy after your classes are set up.

In the educator area, here, teachers can streamline how they oversee classes. Furthermore, since the platform incorporates very well with other Google tools. For example, Drive, Doc, and Calendar, there are bunches of inherent easy routes or shortcuts for classroom management responsibilities. For example, when assignments are posted with due dates, they automatically are added to the class schedule for students to see.

3. Using Google Classroom Assignments

Assignments are an extraordinary method used in gathering student work and providing them with feedback and grades. At the point when you create a task, you can give explicit instructions to that task, a due date, and a subject. In a case when you incorporate a due date for the task, students will have until 11:59 PM on the date to present their work for that assignment. In a situation that they present the work late, Google Classroom, despite everything, acknowledges the task, yet indicates that it was turned in late.

Perhaps the best element of the Google Classroom Assignments is that you can add files to the assignments you create. You can include a document from your PC, a file from Google Drive, a YouTube video, or a link to a Website. One thought is that a business instruction educator can allocate writing briefly on an important individual in the news, and then add a link to a YouTube video of that individual giving a speech.

Students can present any sort of file to your Classroom. Not only would students be able to present their finished work as files, but you can also open them directly from the Classroom and grade them. You can open documents submitted to your Classroom as long as your PC has an Internet association and the software expected to open the file... you don't need to be on your school PC!

For instance, you can assign an exposition, and your students can present their finished articles to an assignment you made in your Google Classroom from any PC that has an Internet association. You would then be able to open the document and grade it on your PC at school or home. This medium gives you additional time during class to concentrate on pushing ahead, instead of sitting around idly gathering work.

4. Communication and Collaboration

One component of Google Classroom is creating collaboration, for example, questions, send announcements, and instant beginning class conversations. Educators can likewise rapidly observe who has or hasn't finished the work, and give immediate, ongoing feedback and grades. Google Classroom makes it easy to monitor student work. Right from the Student Work screen, click on any student's task thumbnail to see real-time advancement.

You can set up what a question is worth point wise, and even permit students to connect. Students can share materials and communicate in the class stream or by email. A simple-to-access platform encourages interaction, even in an online environment, and allows students to gain from each other.

Google Classroom allows you to pose a question inside a particular class. Similarly, as with assignments, you can add documents to the questions you post and can allocate a due date. You can post a short answer or different decision questions for your students to respond to in the Classroom. As students answer a different decision question, Google Classroom organizes the outcomes for that question and then shows you the breakdown of the students' answers progressively. At the point when you click on one of the multi-choice answers, the Classroom shows which students picked that choice.

When students respond to a short answer question, Google Classroom can't classify the outcomes, so it shows student responses. By then, you can remark or reply to every student, and give an evaluation as you see fit.

Notwithstanding making assignments and questions, Google Classroom permits you to create announcements. Students can then respond to your announcements, and you also can respond, thereby making a string. Actually, the whole class can have a discussion dependent on one announcement. By and by, you have the alternative of including a file, a YouTube video, or a connection to an announcement.

Announcements are an extraordinary method to post a reminder about task due dates to your students. You can even schedule announcements to post sometime in the future, which can assist you with remaining sorted out as well as your students. Indeed, even classroom teachers can utilize the announcement feature to post reminders, consent forms for field trips, materials in case students lose them, and the list goes on.

In addition to the students cooperating with each other, educators interacting with singular students can likewise interface with guardians/parents (despite the fact that this is confined to emails). The different interactive mediums may incorporate are: email, post to a stream, private remarks, and feedback.

5. Engagement

Most digital locals are OK with innovation and will be progressively able to take possession of their learning through the utilization of innovation. The classroom gives various approaches to create learning intuitive and communitarian. It offers educators the capacity to separate assignments, incorporate videos and site pages into exercises, and create community-oriented gathering assignments.

It's been demonstrated multiple times that students are locked in by innovation. Google Classroom can assist students with turning out to be and remain occupied with the learning procedure. In a situation where you have students answering questions in the Classroom, different students can remark on these answers and develop thought for the others.

One of the most vital features of Google Classroom is that it permits you to discuss better with your students outside the four walls of a classroom. Formerly, students need to be in the classroom for teachers to ask them a question. But now teachers can do it whenever and anywhere.

Just in case you have a Google Account through your region, the Classroom is simply staying there standing by to assist you with testing and engaging your students. In general, utilizing Google Classroom is certainly advantageous. It can spare you a great deal of time and energy and can assist you to better prepare your students for what's to come. The classroom gives students an introduction to an internet learning system. Numerous school and college programs currently expect students to try out at any rate one online class. Exposure to Google Classroom may assist students with progressing into other learning management system utilized in advanced education.

6. Saves Time

Teachers can create classes, disperse assignments, communicate, and remain organized, all in one place. All the entirety of the students, data, entries, and grades are in one convenient area. For students, all the materials for a class are in one single area. There's no compelling reason to find a book, get your journal, drive to a classroom for a lecture, or print out an article. Instead, you can see the exercise on the web, respond to questions, and even submit work across the board area. Everything remains slick and sorted out along these lines, and time isn't squandered searching for lost classroom materials. Google classroom coordinates and automates the utilization of other Google applications, including docs, slides, and spreadsheets, the way toward managing file distribution, grading, developmental evaluation, and feedback is simplified and streamlined. A few highlights like expert grade to Google Sheets, simpler to update grade point scale, console route for entering grades, sort by name on grading page and so forth., spare educators' time.

7. Differentiating Between Skill Levels

Google Classroom lets you separate different skill levels by setting up the same number of the various classrooms as you'd like. One model may act automatically guided reading projects. You may have two or three groups of students utilizing the program; however, Class A may be at a sixth-grade understanding level, Class B at a fourth-grade understanding level, and Class C at a second-grade understanding level.

With Google Classroom, you can isolate each group, so they work at their own pace, and you can likewise observe all of your students from the same dashboard and sort out who's dealing with what to keep steady over who needs extra assistance and which students exceed expectations in the topic and need all the more of a test.

Through the Classroom, educators are effectively ready to separate instruction for students. Allocating exercises to the entire class, singular students, or groups of students takes only a couple of straightforward steps when making an assignment on the Classwork page.

8. Work Is Never Lost

Google Classroom is cloud-based, and as such, they present professional and credible technology to use in learning conditions as Google applications communicate to "a significant segment of cloud-based venture communication tools utilized all through the professional workforce. All documents transferred by teachers and students are put away in a Classroom folder on Google Drive.

Work in Google Classroom saves automatically and can be accessed from any gadget. Students can work flawlessly in any place they are, without agonizing over cumbersome flash drives, messaging files to and fro, or losing progress because of PC glitch. "I left it at home," and "My PC malfunctioned before I could save," are no longer excuses you'll need to engage.

A few students appear to unendingly have a reason for not turning in their work. You've heard the old "the dog ate my schoolwork" answer; however, a few students take reasons to another level. With an advanced classroom, work is assigned and submitted web-based, which means it cannot be "lost." Online platforms additionally permit guardians to keep steady over what their student finished and what still needs to be wrapped up.

A few schools are additionally using web-based or simply put online learning on snow days as opposed to compelling students to create up cancellation because of an extreme climate. Never again is spring break cut or school still in session for some weeks after it ought to have finished. Rather, the school gives access to internet learning modules with the goal that work proceeds even on days when schools are closed.

9. Mobile-Friendly and Easy Integration with Other Products

Google Classroom can be accessed from any PC by means of Google Chrome or from any mobile device irrespective of platform. Google Classroom is intended to be responsive. It is anything but difficult to use on any mobile device. The classroom works with Google Docs, Calendar, Gmail, Drive, and Forms. Versatile access to learning materials that are appealing and simple to interface with is basic in the present web-connected learning conditions.

With the classroom application, both students and teachers can appreciate the full functionality of Google Classroom on a mobile device. Students get notifications when assignments and announcements are posted, making it simple for them to be well informed of all the latest happenings in the classroom. As an educator, the app empowers you to post from your device either directly from the app or utilizing share-sheet support (that small sharing symbol you touch when you need to share photographs or sites from your phone).

10. Free!

The classroom is free for schools, nonprofits, and people. The classroom contains no advertisements and never utilizes your content or student information for publicizing purposes. What's more, anybody can have access to the various applications that can be integrated with google classroom, for example, Drive, Docs, Spreadsheets, Slides, and so forth, basically by signing up a Google account.

11. Adaptable

This application is effectively available and useable to educators and students in both face to face learning environment and completely online condition. This empowers teachers to explore and impact "flipped instructional methods" all the more effectively just as automate and arrange the dissemination and assortment of assignments and interchanges in various instructional milieus

12. Easy Grading

Reviewing and grading content in a CMS/LMS can be demanding. In any case, Google Classroom saves all student work in a file in Google Drive and arranges them conveniently by task title. This makes it simple for the instructor in surveying every student's work and giving remarks. Utilizing the preview feature in google drive can make assessing student work simple and fast.

Google Classroom has a mobile application that permits the student to submit digital work directly to Google Classroom. The teacher is additionally able to post assignments and announcements from the application. Best is that the application permits the educator to grade and give feedback anyplace whenever.

Chapter 5

Differences between google classroom and its alternatives

Albeit most of the learning management systems share a considerable amount of similarities for all intents and purposes, there are a few differentiating features/highlights between Google classroom and its other options/alternatives. In this chapter, we will discuss some of these differentiating features. And these differences could either be generalized, in terms of all available alternatives, or specific to some alternatives.

With the Classroom, you don't need to veer off from standard Google services for another line of service or study. It's anything but difficult to sign in, post on YouTube, attach documents from Drive, create files in Docs, etc. Also, the familiar Google designs and interfaces that require no additional learning curve; Not at all like alternatives, which require an exceptional learning curve to set up. For instance, Schoology clients report a somewhat steep learning curve or expectation to absorb information.

Also, Google Classroom doesn't permit teachers to create content inside the system. Rather, teachers connect to the content they created in different places, for example, Google Docs. Dissimilar to other alternatives where teachers can create their content in their CMS/LMS. Headings, installed videos, instructional components can be in the CMS/LMS like they generally have. In Google Classroom, on the other hand, the CMS/LMS is intended to create content inside the system known as third party contents. Google Classroom doesn't coordinate quizzing features. Teachers can make a connection to Google Forms, Socrative, Kahoot, or other quiz tools. In any case, these are not local or native to Google Classroom.

Some Google classroom alternatives permit the use of its software to build in-house content, which gives the teacher full imaginative control, editable control over the content. These contents can be shared with other educators or even sold in commercial centers known as basic libraries of training content, for instance, OpenSesame. A portion of these libraries are housed inside LMS platforms where associations or people can post the contents, they've made utilizing an assortment of content authoring tools.

Alternatives such as, office 365 training, contain content creating tools like the Microsoft PowerPoint, for basic slideshows. The Moodle for School bundle incorporates the Big Blue Button for video/web conferencing, Quiz venture for gamification with tests and tests, another gamification module called Level Up that incorporates dynamic checkpoints, Word Count for composing assignments, Chemistry Editor for chemistry assignments, group Choice for group projects, and so on. What's more, others complete content writing tools as

Lectora, which can be utilized to create completely interactive e-learning courses and evaluations.

Another difference is the way that the Classroom is totally free for schools, philanthropies, and people. The classroom contains no advertisements. Despite the fact that Google Classroom is a free assistance for educators and students. In any case, they can't join except if their school has enlisted for the free Google for Education package. Google additionally offers optional products and services, for example, Chromebooks, authoring tools, and expert services. Google Classroom gives boundless access to free and doesn't offer any paid plan.

While alternatives come in bundles or plans. They have the first bundle, which is typically free; however, they have limitations. For instance, a few features of Moodle for Free is that it can be utilized for an unlimited measure of time, it is constrained to up to 50 users and 200 MB of document upload. The Moodle for School bundle has three paid yearly plans: The Mini arrangement costs about $190 USD and has room for up to 100 clients. It incorporates two extra highlights: an advance theme for the account and an additional plug-in pack. The Small plan costs about $380 USD and includes the entirety of the features for the Mini plan; however, it suits up to 200 students and up to 400 MB of file upload. Furthermore, ultimately, the Medium plan costs about $760 USD a year. It permits up to 500 users and up to 1,000 MB of document upload.

Additionally, Office 365 education has three plans; office 365 education A1 which is free with certain limitations. Office 365 education A3; $2.50 every month for students, $3.25 every month for staff. What's more, finally, office 365 education A5; $6 every month for students, $8 every month for month.

Google classroom just doesn't provide offline application support, as everything runs in the browser. Alternatives like moodle, Schoology, office 365 instruction, and so on, have offline provision. For instance, with locally installed versions of the efficiency software, a user can work with local Microsoft tools even without having internet access. Although this offline element just works in the paid plans.

Another remarkable difference one would see between google classroom and options is that Google classroom doesn't have the automated features found in alternatives like moodle, office 365 education, and so on. This is probably the main reason a few people, despite all its other features, do not acknowledge google classroom as a full learning management system (LMS). Automated features incorporate; automated quizzes and tests for students, automated updates that spare students the pressure of having to routinely refreshing requests not to miss significant announcements, automated course enlistment/enrollment, programmed exit at the end of a course, and so forth.

Google Classroom doesn't deal with course enrollment like you would discover in an LMS or CMS. Automated course enrollment feature permits students to automatically enroll for courses, particularly those that are mandatory. And furthermore, toward the finish of a course, students are automatically enrolled for the following course in the automation method known as learning paths. Learning paths are flawless, adding structure to learning programs, and it permits the instructor to dole out numerous courses to students to be finished over some stretch of time. These courses are integrated, and once a student finishes one, the following course in the learning path opens up, and notifications are sent. Learning paths show an educator's pedagogy, which is the workmanship (art) or science of being a teacher. It's generally the methods of guidance or the style utilized by a teacher. The learning paths permits the teacher to consolidate exercises in succession where every activity can build on the result of the past one.

For google classroom, the educators would need to send a course code to the students each time for them to take part in another course toward the end of a finished course.

Another automated feature ailing in the google classroom is the robotized exit of students toward the finish of a course. For google, teachers would need to send a suggestion to students to leave the course.

One useful asset to enhance the progress of children's learning is engaging parents/guardians. A few examine shows that most guardians are keen on helping their youngsters whenever given the correct help. One research project completed by SSAT indicated that what causes the distinction to student's accomplishment is a parental commitment to learning at home and not a parental contribution in classrooms.

Furthermore, this is a distinction between google classroom, and a few alternatives are the absence of parent role. The parent role may permit the guardians to consent to policies on behalf of their underage children. Alternatives to google classroom like moodle, awards guardians/parents with access to see certain data from the school MIS, for example, grades, activity reports, group posts, and blog entries, behavior about their children's teacher. It provides guardians with the entire image of their children's accomplishments.

Additionally, alternatives booster parent's engagement in their children's learning through guiding and supporting the homework exercises. Moodle incorporates an action called "Homework." This feature enables educators to assemble materials and exercises as homework which is presented to both guardians and students

Google classroom creates a platform for educators to invite guardians and parents to sign up for email summaries that incorporate a student's performance, forthcoming, or missed work. Unlike some alternatives that permit guardians and guardians access to check and monitor student's advancement.

Another distinction between Google classroom and alternatives is its Universal device accessibility. Google kicked alternatives back when it came to mobile. Google obviously has a native advantage being the originator of the Android mobile operating system, controlling the operating system itself, but to a great extent affecting the application development ecosystem through the Google Play Store.

Third-party designers can write and release applications autonomously on Android, skipping the Play Store itself, although that is viewed to be dangerous from an IT governance point of view, and furthermore, requires special non-default security settings at the individual gadget level to have the option to install an application from other sources outside Play Store. Despite the fact that alternatives such as Microsoft has as of late released functional renditions of its efficiency applications that incorporate well into the Office 365 condition.

In principle, this likewise gives Google a bit of an edge considering tablet devices for classroom use. Android tablets and Chromebook function admirably locally accessing google Apps like its seamless incorporation with google drive in amazing manners while any Microsoft Apps would require downloading and sending to the device. Anything requiring additional exertion with respect to previously burdened school IT classes will get more investigation. Google classroom likewise works well on iPad.

Another significant contrast between google classroom is the fact that unlike some of its alternatives, Google classroom is not available for business. Google Classroom is only available for education.

Chapter 6

Getting Started

Google Classroom relies on Google Drive, which provides users with online storage with respect to automated documents. Teachers can create and store assignments using Google Classroom, Google Forms, Google Drive, Google Slides, and Google Sheets.

Now, with Google classroom, teachers can make learning with computerized content progressively powerful for students mixing up the kinds of resources you share with your students. Other types of media, links to websites, images, YouTube videos, and screencast can likewise be shared between teachers and students in addition to G Suite tools like Google Docs, and Google Slides. There are a variety of options given to students by some teachers on how to submit their work within Google Classroom. For instance, a student might be offered the choice by the teacher to respond to a reading assignment with just a comment, video clips, or drawing that shows their reveals their thinking.

If you, as a teacher, are looking at creating a center of learning for your student, you should consider using the Google Classroom's Stream page. The Stream is where every one of your students can discover up-coming assignments and announcements, and furthermore the main thing your students see when they sign in.

The Stream is used by some teachers to set up Class conversation sheets, where students can interact online by posting inquiries or remarks on each other's posts. This conversation sheets can assist in the increment of student participation in class and offers the student the medium to have their voice heard (or read) by the class. With discussion, the Stream can be used as a closed social network, and that can be a great way to help these students practice using all kinds of digital citizenship skills in a contained environment type of setting.

Applications and Websites that incorporate with Google Classroom

Hundreds of websites and apps exist that coordinate with Google Classroom. These applications, some of them make and distribute their own outsider additional items in the Chrome Store while others partner with Google. In the event that you are using Google Classrooms widely, coordinating other educational technology tools can be a method for streamlining your instructions. For example, say you need your students to learn some vocabulary words using Quizlet; you can use Google Classroom integration to directly share and assign a particular flashcard set to your class.

Now, let us see what teachers do with Google Classroom.

1. Keep Classes Organized: With Google Classroom, you can create classes, distribute assignments, send feedback, and see everything in one place, a paperless classroom backed up on a cloud.

2. Connect with your students: This platform makes it easier to link students to your classroom. You have the option to add them directly or send them your class code. You can bring in a group from Google Groups.

3. Improve Communication: Students can message the teacher privately or directly ask the rest of the class questions. Also, the teacher can communicate on an individual basis with the student, comment on their assignments, which changes what may generally be single direction correspondence into two-way correspondence.

4. Learning based on Ability: As a teacher, you can determine which class or group gets which assignments, which is also great for individual learning. You will be able to see who has completed the assignment and who is still working.

5. Submit assignments easily: In Google Classroom, attachments such as Google Docs, Google Drive Files, or links can be included in the assignments by the student. Students can even take a photo and attach it to their assignment.

6. Attach Forms to Post: When creating a post, Google Forms can easily be attached to them. If a form is attached to an assignment, and there is no other

work for students to do, the assignment is automatically marked as done.

7. Organize for Students: Each class has a calendar, and when work is being assigned by the teacher, the expected date to have the work submitted is automatically entered to the calendar. Teachers, students can see the schedule in the Classroom or in Google Calendar on their cell phones or computers

8. Reusing of Post: A teacher can again make use of existing posts such as announcements, assignments, and questions from another class, or a current class. The class settings can also be changed by moving any item to the highest point of the Stream to give it priority.

9. Ask and answer a question: This is a great way to access students by posting a short answer question to a student in the class Stream with the options of students being able to edit their own answers and see and reply to that of other classmates.

10. Maintaining Privacy: Google Classroom restricts access to students' work to the teacher and individual student. This not only protects student privacy, but it also deters cheating.

11. Feedback: A note can be posted on the students' assignment with feedback about his or her work while grading it. The students also can remark or pose inquiry back, thereby creating an easy flow of conversation in the classroom.

12. Class or Group Collaboration: The teacher decides the sharing of Documents and whether he or she

wants the student to only view the document or if they can edit it.

13. Get Help during the Process: You can offer guidance, monitor your students' activities, and even offer encouragement while they are working because of Google Classroom.

14. Get Support: It is easy to get support from Google and other teachers by checking out all of their great support resources:

- What is new in the Classroom

- About Classroom

- Frequently Asked Questions

- Google For Education Help Forum

- Google For Education Training Centre

- Google Educator Groups

And as with all things Google, teachers can count on Google Classroom to be accessible on any device.

Chapter 7

How to create and manage a classroom, invite students and teachers

Before you start using Google classroom, make sure that you have a Google account or have one created for you if you don't. You can access Google Classroom by phone or on your computer by visiting classroom.google.com. To navigate Google Classroom, you must

Create your class

Depending on what you teach, you mainly need to create one class, or you create different classes for each subject you teach or each group of students you teach. Now, to create a class, you are going to

- Navigate to classroom.google.com.

- Choose the I am a Teacher option

- You will see a Plus sign (+) At the upper right-right side of your screen, click it.

- Select Create class. If your school does not have a G-suite for an education account, you will be prompted with a message asking your school to sign up for one before you use the service for students. Ignore this prompted message if you are using Google classroom for your own personal use.

Enter the class name, section depending on how many, subject, and room number. When you are done inserting this information, click 'create class', and you're quickly taken to the class page. The section field is a secondary description of your class. This is where you add something like 1st period, a grade level, or some other short description.

Inviting Students to your class

Once you are done creating your class, the next thing is to invite your students. This you can do in the following ways. The first is to invite students via email (manually)

This can be done by:

- Clicking the class, you want to invite student into

- Navigate the People tab.

- Click the Invite students' icon.

- A search box would then be brought up in which you can look for the email address of each student.

- Once you're done adding, click Invite. This will email notification to your students with a link inviting them to join your online class. This one method teachers typically skip because it is labor-intensive.

Inviting students via Classroom code: Another way of inviting students to your class and a much easier way to accomplish this is by having students join on their own via a class code. The class code is used by the students to join your class if you provide them with it. It is a short code and to access it,

- Go to Google classroom,
- Click the Class Setting icon.
- You will find the class code. Write it down or better still copy it and share the code with your students however you'd like.
- Students then navigate to classroom.google.com, click the + sign and select Join at the upper right side of the screen.
- Students enter the class code and will right away become a member of the class.

Note: The teacher can disable or change the class code at any time. Simply click the drop-down that's located next to the class code and disable or reset it as you desire. This action will not affect the students who are already registered.

Inviting teachers to your class

You can invite the teacher to your class to help coordinate class activities. If you use used Google group, you can welcome another group of co-teachers simultaneously to.

Your G Suite administrator may just permit teachers and students from your school to join classes. In the event that you need to include a teacher from another school, contact your admin to update your domain's class membership settings.

To invite a co-teacher to teach your class:

- Go to classroom.google.com
- Click class to add co-teachers or groups to.
- Hover your mouse over the People tab.
- Click Invite teachers.
- Enter the email address (es) of the teacher you are inviting or group of teachers you want to join your class. Classroom shows matching addresses to look over from the list of addresses as you enter the text.
- From the search results, then click a teacher or group.
- To invite more teachers or groups is optional (repeat steps 5-6)
- Click invite.

Accepting an invitation to co-teach a class

Invited teachers get an email requesting or asking them to co-teach your class. To join the class, the teacher invited clicks the email link and click Accept.

Also, there are some few permissions co-teacher(s) needs to be aware of:

- The Primary or main teacher has the sole right to delete the class
- Co-teachers cannot be removed or unenrolled by the Primary teacher from the class.
- Muting of teachers is not allowed
- The class Google Drive folder is with the Primary teacher.

- After joining the class, the co-teachers also have access to the class Google Drive Folder.

Edit, move or archive a class

For ones' first time of sampling out Google Classroom, you may end up creating some test classes just to get the hang of it and also to see how it works, and it offers. This is how to edit and delete your test class when you are done sampling it.

- Click on the menu button at the upper left side of the screen. It looks like three on horizontal lines
- Select Class to enable you to see the classes you have created
- Sets of dots on the upper right side of the class you want to make partial changes should be selected
- To make the needed changes, select Move, Edit, or Archive

Note: Click on the Edit button if you want to change the section or rename your class, subject, or room number. The Move button is for rearranging the classes order in your dashboard. The Archive button is to remove the class from your dashboard and archive it. You can access an Archive class through the settings by clicking on the menu icon and selecting Archived Classes. An Archived class can be restored here or permanently delete them.

Altering how your class looks

You are given an original layout picture right when your class is created. When students click on your group to get announcements and assignments, this is the picture they will see. This image can be customized to suit your class with a few quick steps:

Changing Theme

- On the banner image, hover your mouse

- At the bottom right side, look for Select Theme link

- You can open your photo gallery and select a theme for your class

- To change the original image that came with the creation of your class, Select Theme from your photo gallery

There, you will find an assortment of pictures to browse from; however, most themes you will find are on the scholastic subject. For example, you could pick books for Language Art Classes, a piano for Music, a hued pencil for Art, etc. You can likewise transfer your photograph by tapping the Upload photograph link.

Add a Syllabus to Google classroom

A teacher can create and allocate work for their students through the help of Google Classroom. Worksheets, questions, essays can be shared and made available online to your class in a paperless format.

Navigate to the Classwork tab

- Click Create and then choose questions and materials. You can also view all current and also past assignments.

- Add a title, description, and any other attachments you desire for your class.

- Click Topic and then assign your materials to a new topic called Syllabus

- Click on Post when you are done.

Materials can be assigned to multiple classes if needed or even to individual students. You can choose the alternative you need from the upper left-hand corner when you are creating another material for your class.

If you want your syllabus topic to be on top of your class page, select the arrows at the upper right side of the topic, and select Move Up. You can repeat as often as necessary. Another way to get this done is to relocate Topics or Materials by clicking and hauling up and down on the Classwork page.

Assignment creation in Google classroom

Assignments can be created and also assigned to students, right from Google Classroom, and here are some useful options for teachers to take advantage of:

Go to the class you want to add the assignment to

At the extreme top of the page, Click the Classwork tab.

Now click the Create button, then select Assignment or Question if you like to pose a single question to your students.

Give a title to your assignment and include any additional description or instructions in the box below.

The due date for your assignment should be chosen by clicking Date, and then add a time frame in the event that you need to determine when it is due on that given day.

Choose the Assignment type you want to create by tapping on the symbol close to the word Assign. Your choices are to either upload a file from your computer, add a YouTube video, attach a file from Google Drive, or add a link to a website.

Click Assign once you have completed the form. An email notification message would be sent to your students, letting them know about the assignment. For future reference, you can schedule the assignment to be saved and be posted later. It can be posted to multiple classrooms by clicking the name of the class on the assignment window at the upper left-hand corner and pick the entirety of the classes that you need to relegate it to. All the assignments are gathered by Google Classroom and automatically added to your Calendar, which from the Classwork tab, you can easily click the calendar icon to get a better overall view of the timeline for the due dates of all your assignments.

Also, while creating an assignment, there may frequently be times when you need to append an archive from Google Docs. These can be useful while giving protracted directions, study guides, and other materials. When attaching these types of files, you'll make sure you chose the correct setting for how your students can interact with it. A drop-down menu will appear as soon as you're done attaching one to the assignment with the following three options:

- **Students can view files:** This option is to be used the teacher wants only the students to view files and not to make any changes to it. This is perfect for study and nonexclusive gifts that the entire class needs access to.

- **Students can Modify/edit file:** This option is to be used when the document provided by you needs to be worked on in groups as an in-class project or on an individual basis, where students may be working on individual slides in the same Google

Presentation, or where they are cooperatively conceptualizing thoughts for your next class topic.

- **Make a separate copy for each student:** This option is used to create a separate copy of the same document for the students in the class to complete and give them permission to edit the file. The original copy that belongs to the teacher remains untouched, and access to it by the student is restricted. This option is to be chosen if you prefer to quickly disseminate a paper that has a digital worksheet template where students are to fill in the blanks with their own answers or an essay question for students to work on.

Using topics to organize and group assignments

You can use topics to group and sort assignments and materials together using the Classwork tab. This is also a better way for teachers and students to find the assignments they are looking for. To do this,

- Navigate to your Class
- Click the Classwork tab.
- Click on the Create button
- Then select Topic.
- Click Add after you are done selecting a Name for your Topic. This is to help compartmentalize work into the various units you teach throughout the session and to split your content by type breaking it down into classwork, assignment, readings, and other topic areas.

From the assignment creation screen, the teacher can include new assignments to a Topic. Next to the Topic, select the drop-down box and then assign it. If your assignments have already been created, then move to Topic, and from the classwork tab,

- Hover your mouse over the assignment to be move
- You will see three dots, click on it
- Choose Edit
- A drop-down box will appear, right next to Topic
- Click the drop-down box and choose the Topic you need to move it to.

Google Forms with Google classroom

This form is used to create many things, such as surveys, quizzes, feedback, and even sign-ups forms. We will be looking at how this form is used to create a variety of questions for the students as quizzes. The first thing to do in creating quizzes is to create a basic form. Navigate to Google Forms homepage, and click on the blank icon, change the form's settings. Click the quizzes tab and switch this to a quizzes button on presenting several quizzes options available to choose from. Now you choose the best way your students can interact with your quizzes.

Click Save once your desired settings have been chosen. You can then assign a name to your quiz and start setting your questions.

How to select the right answers for your questions

To specify the right answers to each of your quiz questions, click the Answer Key. The screen will appear differently based on the question type chosen, so let's see how to choose the correct answer to the various question types we have:

- **For Multiple-choice or check-box questions:** The correct answer or answers from the available choices given should be chosen.

- **For a short-answer question:** This is when the answer is typed in the Add a correct answer box. Multiple correct answers may also be added if the wording varies for a particular question. Mark all other answers incorrect should be checked off, which automatically marked answers that don't match, and any answers that aren't exact match will be left for you to review manually and grade only if it's left unchecked.

- **Paragraph question:** These are questions that don't offer the opportunity of adding correct answers. Reason being that they require more analysis and are longer. You will have to read each individually and grade them on your own.

After choosing the correct answers, you use point field to select how many points you're awarding for each question.

Answer feedback is another option to employ. This gives the students feedback on certain questions depending on whether they chose the correct answer. Click the Answer feedback, and the message that should appear for the correct or incorrect answers be typed. You can preview your questions when you're done to make sure everything is correct. To carry out this action, click on the Preview icon on the upper right side.

How students complete and submit assignments

By signing into Google Classroom, students can see an active assignment by clicking on the class they belong to and review upcoming assignments. However, there is a better way to go about this. At the top left side of the screen, hover your mouse on the menu button. Select To-do from the pop-up menu showing the students a list of assignments for all their classes, as well as the ones they have turned in, the ones that are outstanding and the one long over-due. Assignments that are graded by teachers would also be shown with their grade point value close to them.

Hovering your mouse on these assignments, a relevant file for the student would be opened with an extra button seen if it is a Google Drive File On the toolbar next to the share button. The markings on this button is "Turn it in." On clicking it, the students' assignment will be submitted to the teacher.

Adding sections to your quiz

To have your questions broken up across various pages instead of them all appearing on a single page depending on how many they are, you can make use of Sections.

To do this, in the toolbar on the side, click the Add section icon. You can also include questions to these sections following the same instructions listed above. Also, questions can be moved to other sections dragging and dropping them using the icon shown below.

Adding Quizzes to class

Once you're done creating your quiz, you need to bring it over to your class. Also, forms can be attached just like how you attach documents, linked to your assignment.

- When creating an assignment on the lower-left corner Click on the Google Drive icon,
- Click on the quiz you have created.
- Click Add.

After the quiz attached to the assignment has been sent out, your students will be able to complete it.

Grading, Review, and Return of Assignments

In Google classroom, as students begin working on assignments, you can view how far they have gone and add comments or edit the document. When the assignments have been submitted, you can give a numeric grade and return it to the student. Since Google Classroom gave each assignment its own page, it will be easy to grade and leave feedback for your students. The students would be notified via email if your school has email set up for them or will receive a message when next they log in to Google Classroom. You can also return an assignment without grades.

To view student's work, go to

- Classroom.google.com
- Navigate to the Classwork tab
- The assignment to grade, select it.
- Then click view Assignment

This brings up the Student assignment Page for the assignment. The student assignment page will show the current status of students' work for the assignment. This is where you'll be able to view each of the students' submission and grade them. The following can be reviewed on the student work page:

- The number of students who submitted work and who didn't.

- Done- these are a list of students who submitted their work.

- Not Done- these are a list of students who haven't submitted their work

- Thumbnails- this is the reduced size version of the work submitted by students.

To add a private comment, click the students' names on the left, click the Add private comment, enter a comment, and then click post. To also add a comment to the class, at the Top, select instructions, click Add class comment, enter a comment and then click post.

Grading an assignment

To grade an assignment, next to the student's name, click Add grade, on the student Work page, and enter the grade. You can decide to get done with reviewing and return the assignments to the students during another meeting. Notwithstanding, private remarks entered during reviewing won't be saved except if you return the assignment to the students.

The original point value for each assignment which is 100, this can be changed by clicking the drop-down arrow and select a point value. Input the point value of your choice, or select Ungraded, and click Update.

Returning an Assignment

The box next to each student whose assignment you want to return should be checked off and click Return. Adding a private comment to the student is optional. Then click Return again to confirm.

Changing and Exporting of Grades

The Grades on an assignment can be changed after it's returned to a student. To do this, go through the same steps as above. When you have to change the grade, check the box next to each student whose assignment you want to return, and then click Return.

To view the grades of the students in the class at a glance, they should be exported from Classroom to Google Sheets or to a comma-separated value (CSV) file. For assignments, you've completed the process of grading, click the gear icon at the upper right-hand, on the Student Work page, and select Copy all grades to Google Sheets to export the grades. When you've created one of these spreadsheets, note that it won't update naturally, and you'll have to send out the grades again at whatever point you grade more assignments.

Communicating with students and Parents

Emailing your students

With the help of Google Classroom, it is conceivable to email your students, regardless of whether it's a message to one student specifically or the whole class. In respective of the student you would prefer to email, the first place you need to navigate is the People tab. Depending on who you're emailing, you have various options here like:

- **Emailing a single student:** Find this students' name, click More button, and select Email student.

- **Emailing multiple students:** click off the names of the students you'd like to email, then click Action and then select the Email.

- **Emailing the entire class:** Check the box located above the list of students to select them all. Click Action and select Email

Posting announcements

You can post announcements to the class' stream. The Stream tab houses all of the activities that have taken place within your classroom, such as any announcements or assignments you have posted as a teacher and any post or comments from students if permitted them with the most recent appearing at the top. You can easily post announcements or attachments to the stream page by clicking and then sharing in your class box. You can either choose to type a message to your students, attach from your Google Drive or computer files, You Tube videos or links can be brought in, and then post directly to your stream. At a precise date and time, you can also schedule the post to be sent out or save as a draft to post at a later time. By clicking the drop-down menu next to the student sections, you can also choose to share this announcement with every student in the class, or you can select a specific student.

Click the Stream tab to post an announcement. At the highest point of the stream that reads Share something with your class, click the feed. You can easily type whatever you want and then include a link or attachment if so desired from here. Click Post once you're done.

Class Summaries for Parents

Parents and guardians of students can now get email outlines via Google Classroom. These include recent class activity, missing work, and upcoming work. These summaries are automatically generated and cannot be altered to suit each individual with additional content. Parents or guardians get to choose whether they receive these emails daily or weekly, or not at all. Note that Class summaries are only available when your students are using Google powerful online tools. Also, access must be granted to teachers by school administrators as touching these email summaries.

Chapter 8

How to assign and manage homework and assignments

Overview

Assignments are a useful tool on Google Classroom for delivering, tracking, and also grading student submissions. Even submissions that are non-electronic can also be tracked using the Assignments tool.

Add an Assignment

Creating an Assignment:

- Open classroom.google.com.
- At the top, click on Class and open Classwork.
- Also, click on Create and click on Assignment.
- Input the title and necessary instructions.

Posting Assignment:

a. To one or more classes:

- Just below For, click the drawdown on Class.
- Choose the Class you want to include.

b. To individual students:

- Select a class and click the drawdown on All Student
- Uncheck All Student
- Then select the particular student(s)

Inputting grade category:

- Click the drawdown on Grade Category
- Select Category
- Edit the following (Optional):
- Click Grades to edit the grades page
- Click Instructions to compose the Assignment
- Click Classwork to create a homework, quiz, and test

Change the point value:

- Click the drawdown below Points
- Create a new point value or click ungraded

Edit due date or Time:

- Click on the drawdown below Due
- Click on the dropdown on No due date
- Fix date on the Calendar
- Create due Time by clicking Time, input a time adding AM or PM

Add a topic:

- Click on the drawdown below Topic
- Click on Create topic and input the topic name
- Click on an existing Topic to select it

Insert Attachments:
File:

- Click on Attach
- Search for the file and select it
- Click Upload

Drive:

- Click on Drive
- Search for the item and click it
- Click Add

YouTube:

- Click on YouTube
- Type in the keyword on the search bar and click search
- Select the video
- Click Add

For video link by URL:

- Click on YouTube and select URL
- Input the URL and Add

Link:

- Click on Link
- Select the URL
- Click on Add link

You can delete an attachment:

- Click remove or the cross sign beside it.

You can also determine the number of students that interacts with the Attachment:

- Click on the drawdown besides the Attachment
- Select the required option:
- Students can View File– This implies that students are allowed to read the data but cannot edit it.
- Students can edit the file – This means students can write and share the same data.
- Make a personal copy of each student – This means students can have their transcript with their name on the file and can still have access to it even when turned in until the teacher return it to them.

Note: If you encounter an issue like, no permission to attach a file, click on copy. This will make Classroom make a copy, which is attached to the Assignment and saved to the class Drive folder.

Add a Rubric:

You must have titled the Assignment before you create a rubric

- Click the Add sign beside Rubric
- Click on Create rubric
- Turn off scoring by clicking the switch to off, besides the Use scoring
- Using scoring is optional, click Ascending or Descending beside the Sort the order of points.

Note: using scoring, gives you the room to add performance level in any, with the levels arranged by point value automatically.

- You can input Criterion like Teamwork, Grammar or Citations. Click the criterion title
- Add Criterion description (Optional). Click the Criterion description and input the description

Note: You can add multiple performance level and Criterion

- Input points by entering the number of points allotted

Note: The total rubric score auto-updates as points are added

- Add Level title, input titles to distinguish performance level, e.g., Full Mastery, Excellent, Level A
- Add Descriptions, input expectations for each performance level
- Rearrange Criterion by clicking More and select Up or Down
- Click Save on the right corner to save Rubric

Reuse Rubric:

- Click on the Add sign beside Rubric
- Click Reuse Rubric
- Enter Select Rubric and click on the title. You can select Rubric from a different class by entering the class name OR by clicking the drawdown and select the Class.

- View or Edit rubric, click on preview, click on Select and Edit to edit, save changes when done. Go back and click Select to view

View rubric assignments:

- Click on Rubric
- Click the arrow up down icon for Expand criteria
- Click the arrow down up icon for Collapse criteria

The grading rubric can be done from the Student work page or the grading tool.

Sharing a Rubric:

This is possible through export. The teacher creates the Rubric exports, and these are saved to a class Drive called Rubric Exports. This folder can be shared with other teachers and imported into their Assignment.

The imported Rubric can be edited by the teacher in their Assignment, and this editing should not be carried out in the Rubric Exports folder.

Export:

- Click on Rubric
- Click More on the top-right corner and enter Export to Sheets
- Return to Classwork page by clicking close (cross sign) at the top-left corner
- At the top of the Classwork page, click on Drive folder and enter My Drive

- Select an option, to share one rubric, right-click the Rubric. To share a rubric folder, right-click on the folder.
- After right-clicking, click on Share and input the e-mail you are sharing to.
- Then click Send

Import:

- Click on the Add sign beside Rubric and enter Import from Sheets
- Click on the particular Rubric you want and click on Add
- Edit the Rubric (Optional)
- Click on Save

Editing Rubric Assignment:

- Click on the Rubric
- Click on More at the top-right corner and enter Edit
- Click Save after making changes

Deleting Rubric Assignment:

- Click on the Rubric
- Click on More at the top-right corner and enter Delete
- Click Delete to confirm

Posting, Scheduling, or Saving Draft Assignment:
Post:

- Open Classwork and click on Assignment
- Click on the drawdown beside Assign, on the top-right corner
- Click on Assign to post the Assignment

Schedule:

- Click on the drawdown beside Assign, on the top-right corner
- Enter Schedule
- Input the and date you want the Assignment posted
- Click Schedule

Save:

- Click on the drawdown beside Assign, on the top-right corner
- Enter Save Draft
- Editing Assignment:
- Open Classwork
- Click on More (three-dot) close to Assignment and enter Edit
- Input the changes and save for posted or schedule assignment, while Go to Save draft, to save the draft assignment

Adding Comments to Assignment:

- Open Classwork
- Click Assignment and Enter View Assignment
- Click on Instructions at the top
- Click on Add Class Comment
- Input your comment and Post

To Reuse Announcement and Assignment:

Announcement:

- Open the Class
- Select Stream
- Slide into the Share something with your class box and click on a square clockwise up and down arrow or Reuse post

Assignment:

- Open Classwork and click on Create
- Click on a square clockwise up and down arrow or Reuse post
- Select the Class and Post you want to reuse
- Then click on Reuse

Delete an Assignment:

- Open Classwork
- Click on More (three-dot) close to Assignment
- Click on Delete and confirm the Delete

Creating a Quiz Assignment:

- Open Classwork and click on Create
- Click Quiz Assignment
- Input the title and instructions
- You can switch on Locked mode on Chromebooks to ensure student can't view other pages when taking the quiz
- You can switch on Grade Importing to import grades

Response and Return of Grades:

Response:

- Open Classwork
- Click on Quiz Assignment and free Quiz Attachment
- Click on Edit and input Response

Return:

- Open Classwork
- Click on Quiz Assignment
- Pick the student and click on Return
- Confirm Return

Chapter 9

Tools, Extensions and Other Features
for Both Teachers and Students

Tools

There are numerous tools that are available on google classroom for both students and teachers to enhance excellent communication and improve the teaching and learning process. However, these tools are only currently available on mobile apps. These tools allow one to write and draw on an assignment; you can even highlight text, underline words, leave a note, and also draw shapes.

Writing and Drawing tool

This tool allows you to draw and write notes, below are some of the type of files you can draw and write on.

1. Google Docs, Slides and Sheets

2. Microsoft Office documents

3. JPEG or GIF

4. Adobe PDF

How to use the Write Tool:

- Click on Classroom and Open Class
- Select the Assignment and open the file you want to write on
- You tap to open an already existing file attached to the document
- Click on Add Attachment to open a new file and upload it, then tap to open
- At the upper right side, click on Edit to open the note tool
- You can write any note or draw
- Tap More (three vertical dots) and click save for Android devices, while click save for iOS devices
- You can discard your changes, tap on Back (backward arrow) and click Discard

Note: On saving the new document, both Google Docs file and Microsoft Office document are saved as a separate PDF document, while for a JPEG or PNG image file and PDF, it saves as an edited file, and it replaces the original.

Using the Tools

For writing and drawing on notes, the tools below are what you need; they can be found at the base of the screen.

Select – For selecting notes to resize and move

Erase – Erasing notes

Write – Writing or drawing lines with a pen

Mark – Writing or drawing lines with a marker

Highlight – Highlighting texts or images

Add text – Adding of a text note

- To engage the write, highlight and mark tools, double tap on them, while the select, erase, and add text is just a click.

- When you double-tap, you can change the colors. Click on the dropdown arrow to access all the colors and sizes

- Select any color and size of a pen for writing, highlighting, or marking.

- To add a text note, click add text, place your finger on the screen and drag to create a text field, then input your message

- You can change the text box size, click on the edge of the text box and drag to suit the size you want. Also, you can resize the text by selecting the text and expanding or decreasing it with your fingers

Erasing Marks

- Click on Erase

- Select a mark you want to erase and click it

- You can also erase all marks on the page by double-clicking Erase

- Click on Clear page

Move a note or image

- Add an image

- Click Select or the edge of the image

- Using your finger, drag the image to move it

Zooming on a Note

- Place two of your fingers on the note and drag them out to Zoom in

- Place two of your fingers on the note and drag them together to Zoom out

- Place two of your fingers on the note and drag them across to Pan over

Undo and Redo

- Click on Undo (a curved arrow facing the left) immediately to cancel an action. You can likewise click it more than once, thus canceling out consecutive actions

- Click on Redo (a curved arrow facing the right) immediately to redo an action. You can click it more than once, just like undo, but this time it would **redo** consecutive actions

Google tools useful for Classroom

Google Drive

This is cloud storage of about 15GB that allows users to store up all data without a charge, but you should have an internet connection to access them. This is a fantastic tool that stores divers types of files, including PDF files, audio, images, videos, documents etc., you simply need to upload it, and then it's safe and secure.

Another thing you need to know about Google Drive is the ability to link up with others, sharing files, sharing them with your students to download, view, and create their files to a central folder, and you can share with other teachers as well, even students to student. This is the best form of file organization for pupils, their parents, or even your colleagues to access.

Just when you are thinking, I always have to be online to view my files or data, boom; you can access your files offline by setting your Google Drive offline. Nice right? Yea, I know.

Google Docs

This is different from Google Drive, as some persons assume. This is the same with Microsoft Word, except that it is free and online, you must have an internet connection to access it. The high side of this tool is its ability for students to do a collaborative assignment without the regular transferring of documents. They can all access the same report online and its in-built chatting module. Also, it takes us to the paperless age, where we do not have to write on papers.

Google Forms

This tool is so cool, it helps you create a pop quiz and carryout other assessments, and it is self-grading. It is most advisable to use this tool with Flubaroo as add-ons, it helps assign the tests to specific students, records their response, and send results through e-mails to students and their parents. It is free

Set-up:
- Open your Google Drive and then create a new Form
- Click on New and open More
- Click on Google Forms
- Input the instructions and the answer keys

- You should install Flubaroo, to enhance its functionality
- Click on Add-ons, and Open Get add-ons

Google CS First

The Google CS First is a program for computer science, designed to equip children between age 9-14 years, with the proper skill to face the future. All materials are available to teach students with no experience at all of computer science. This tool is great for teachers in schools to use in teaching their students because the result will be overwhelming.

Hangouts on Air

With just your webcam, computer, and an internet connection, you can host a live broadcast with Hangouts on Air. This tool allows you to host a guest speaker for your Classroom, which allows your pupils to interact and ask questions. If, as a teacher, you are collaborating with other teachers, then this is your tool. You can also record the live broadcast, which you either save as private or public on YouTube video.

Google Maps

This is the most used mapping tool online, drivers use it for directions, and it gives an all-round view of any location in the world. It is employed as a virtual atlas in the Classroom but functions best when paired with Panoramio to produce stunning images. Studying geography just became better and more fun.

Google Earth

This tool gives a 3D pictorial view of the Earth, very handy in geography, social studies, and history explorations. It offers students a virtual trip to everywhere in the world, even outside this world, zooming in on Mars, the Moon and farther galaxies. Amazingly, it can be employed in significant disciplines like computing math equations and understanding marine biology.

YouTube

This tool can also be useful for teachers, as they can access some educational videos to support their lesson plans. Below are some helpful YouTube channels to subscribe to:

- TedED
- The School of Life
- BrainCraft
- Crash Course
- AsapSCIENCE
- Life Noggin

Google+

Most online teachers make use of Google+ because it is Google's social media handle, where people link up with one another, which creates a community network amongst teachers, giving them the privilege to share ideas and support one another. If you are a tutor, here are some community you should check out:

- Educators on Google+
- Google Classroom Educators
- Google Science Fair
- Made with Code
- Education
- Connected Classrooms
- National Geographic Education
- Google Education
- Chromebook EDU
- Science Teaching Resources
- TED on Google Plus

Google Calendar

It can be instrumental if you know how to use it. Organization of activities and time management is always an issue, but with this Google Calendar, you are sure to have your daily schedule, reminders, and to-do list well planned, all you need do is to create it. It can help you schedule a parent-teacher conference, and also for your lesson planning.

Google Sites

You can also take advantage of Google Sites, to share your content not just to your students alone, but to your colleagues and even parents. There are lots you can do with Google Sites, but here are a few:

- Posting of announcements
- Publishing of classroom rules
- Information on upcoming events
- Create a wiki for class projects
- Uploading and sharing files
- Post materials for reading
- Introduce monthly topics or themes
- Curriculum resources sharing

Apps Compatible with Google Classroom

Apps have become an integral part of our everyday life; there is almost a software or an app for everything we do. So, it's wise to acknowledge and also be exposed to some Apps that work with Google Classroom. These are a few Apps that I believe are necessary for maximum exploration of Google Classroom for both teachers and students.

Writable App

This is a writing platform that helps students become better writers by supporting teachers in the assessment and monitoring of students writing growth; it also aids teachers in prep and grading and allows them the time to focus on their writing instructions. It partners Google Classroom and Google Docs to generate the best platform for students and teachers, through speed up grading, reveals students who need improvement, writing monitoring programs and exporting grades to sheets, learning management systems, and Google Classroom.

Abre App

The Abre provides an Educational Management App, which grants access to means of communication like announcements, content-specific channels, and headlines. With one single click, you can access all web-based software of a school. This is a single software that connects other apps software to provide critical functionality for Learning Management, School and Classroom Management, and Data and Analytics. This is actually what beautifies the App, the ability to be used singly and in a combined form.

Actively Learn

This is a platform that provides the opportunity for students to be well-read and vast in any field. This is designed to be an auxiliary tool for teachers to give students in-depth knowledge, by providing material and documents on all areas of learning, it is tagged 'content library.' It also allows a student to import personal content and assign articles that are in line with the objectives of learning.

Additio App

This App is designed for performance assessment, and it helps in rubric assessment, standards-based grading, lesson planning, and tracking of attendance or custom report creation. It allows the family to assess their kid's progress and involve them in learning too. It aids teachers is sending notifications and student's grades directly to their phones.

Adobe Spark App

This App is designed for creating narrated videos, writing assignments, presentations, posters, and divers' creative visual content. This App is not streamlined to Educational purposes alone, and can also be employed to promote personal business and content.

Relay App

This App secures privacy and data guidelines and aid schools in critical decision making to improve ROI and drive adoption. Amazingly, it works on all devices, and can identify any App, view all activities, and is very easy to operate.

AppWriter App

This is designed to help a student in English, both in speaking and in writing. The App is divided into six main functions, as follows.

Text to Speech – This App is equipped with the purpose of reading out texts when highlighted, with speed, unique voices, and its speed can be adjusted.

Audio File – Texts can be selected, and a download file created and played

Predictive text – Grammar and spelling of students can be improved, as the App suggests the next possible word to a student

Statistics – It stores up information like common mistakes and other relevant data; it can be accessed later.

PDF Editor – It allows comments and answers to questions directed to the PDF document by both students and teachers.

Snipping tool – It provides the means to read, copy, paste, and other functions by scanning images and fetching texts in them.

ASSISTments App

This App allows teachers to assign whatever they want, whenever they want, for free. It also allows for flexibility in digitalizing and creating content. For students, this helps them with their Assignment, gives them feedback in real-time, and aids them in the revision of their work. This also provides feedback to teachers and allows them to analyze trends in the Class to improve teaching. Teachers and students always fall for their flexibility in meeting needs and helping them achieve effectiveness, plus it's so compatible with Google Classroom.

Autodesk Tinkercad App

This is a 3D design app. It enables a student to design 3D, code-blocks, and circuits. It is highly recommended for younger pupils, as it prepares them for future diversion into the world of Engineering. This is an excellent tool you and easily link with Google Classroom and with a single click, create assignments, and turn them in.

Backpack App for Google Drive

This App helps showcase digital portfolios, and helps student curate, reflect on, and advertise digital artifacts for districts employing G Suite for EDU. It controls the sharing and artifacts organization in Google Drive, and it perfectly links with Google Classroom.

Key Features and Their Benefits
Time Saving Feature

Ease Adding Student – With a code, students can join a class. The teacher is afforded the time to concentrate on teaching.

Managing Multiple Classes – The ability to reuse the same material for other classes by simply sharing them.

Co-teaching – You are afforded the privilege to tutor together with up-to 20 other instructors for a course.

Enriching Assignment – You can enrich your assignments by adding materials like videos from YouTube, Google survey forms, PDF, and files from Google Drive. Highlighting, natation, and drawing are possible via the Classroom Mobile App.

One-Click Worksheets – A copy of an assignment can be made by one click, and worksheets can be attached.

Customizing Assignments – You can adjust an Assignment as you want. You can add due dates, points, topic, and grade categories.

Individual Assignments – Assignment can be sent individually to all or selected students in a class.

Prepare in Advance – Assignments, questions, and announcements can be scheduled or drafted for later posting.

Quick Exit Tickets and Polling – Questions posted to students can be results viewed within the Classroom.

Customize Your Class Graphics – You can make your Class look fancy, by changing the theme or color.

Keep Resources in One Place – Topics are created for critical resources, to allow students access materials like online texts, class syllabus, or office hour sign-up sheets.

Organization – Google Calendar for classes helps prep students as they get updates on upcoming events. Teachers' class review is done with ease because sorting them out is easy.

Customize Grading – This can be achieved by choosing a grading system, and create the grade category, view the grades page to see grading.

Integrate Other Favorite Teaching Tools – You can link your already existing Classroom with partner Apps.

Communicating and Collaborating Features

Full Access – Classrooms are accessible anytime and anywhere, through the web or mobile Apps.

Real-Time Feedback – The Docs grading provides immediate viewing, commenting, and editing of student's work.

Create Class Discussion – You can post topics on the stream page to engage the students in a discussion and encourage them to reply one another.

Manage Class Discussions – You can control who posts on the stream page by muting students.

Sharing Content – Classroom extension can be employed in sharing videos, links, and images from websites. You can also push sites to the screen of students.

Communicating with Guardians – Parents and guardians can be invited by teachers via the G Suite domain by sending them an e-mail so that they can receive summaries of student's work.

Easy Support for Administrators

Affordable and Secure – It is safe from ads as every data is secure and not shared for advertising purposes.

Simple Sign–in – With just a click, both teachers and students can sign into Classroom with G Suite for Education accounts.

Set Permissions – You can set up restrictions on teachers, on who can and cannot create or manage Classroom.

Student Information System (SIS) Integration – The Classroom API is used to set-up classes and student rosters using the SIS. If students participate in the beta program, grades can be added to the SIS from the Classroom.

Professional Development – Visit the Google Training Center for training on google classroom.

Personal Data Protection – This strictly adhere to FERMA compliance with rights and privacy.

Latest Updated Features

Updates and new features are regularly included in the Classroom. Below are some of the latest since January 2019.

April 2020 - In this month, Google unleashed a new feature of video meetings.

Class Video Meetings

This is possible through Google Meet, as teachers kick-start the video meeting for a student to join. Students cannot create the meet, and the Admin set-up determines what becomes of the Meet in terms of restriction and permissions. Most notably, if a teacher is to exit the Meet, the Meet comes to an end.

How to set-up

This can only be carried out by the Admin of a school, while teachers and students are to login.

1. Turn on Meet video call

- Open Google Admin console and Sign in
- Click on Apps, open G Suite, and click Hangout Meets and Google Hangouts.
- Check the top if Hangout service is ON for everyone, if not, then follow these steps:
- Click the dropdown arrow close to service status
- Click ON for everyone and save
- Then set-up who can start up Meet and other settings
- Open Hangouts Meet and Google Hangouts
- Click on Meet settings
- Pick-out an organizational unit that includes faculty and staff or the Classroom Teachers group if verified.
- At the top right, click on the gray box, and click on Edit

- Check the box close to the Let users place video and voice calls.
- Click on save

2. Turn on Live stream

- Click on Stream
- Choose either a configuration group or a child organizational unit to apply the setting for all.
- Check the box for Let people stream their meetings.
- Then click Save. An organizational unit or group gives you the ability to override or inherit a parent organizational unit, or to unset a group.

3. Turn on Meeting Record

This feature is recommended to be enabled for faculty and staff or the Classroom Teachers group with verified teachers only, but if you must include faculty and students, then you should create a separate organizational unit with separate access rules.

- Click on Recording.
- Check the box for Let people record their meetings.
- Then click save. An organizational unit or group gives you the ability to override or inherit a parent organizational unit, or to unset a group.

Viewing the Meet Feature Available to a User or Group

To ensure its only specific users that can access the recording and live streaming features, go to settings and see what's turned on or off for a particular user, organizational unit, or Google Group.

- Open Google Hangouts
- Expand Meet Setting by clicking on it, this shows the features that are turned off or on
- Click on option on the left
- Click on Users to search for individual users by their username. Add individual users to organizational unit or group with the proper setting, in case it's on the wrong Meet setting because the Meet setting for individual users cannot be changed.
- Click on group to search for the group name or e-mail. Click on setting name and change the setting, then click on Override.
- Click on the Organizational unit to search for the organizational unit. Click on setting name and change the setting, then click on Override.

It can take within 18 to 24 hours for the change to be effective, but it typically takes a few minutes.

Features and Tips for Teachers

- For accounts set-up for education, the right to mute or remove video meet participants rests on the meeting creator. This prevents the student from attempting to remove their colleague or the teacher.
- If audio quality and internet reception is poor, the camera should be turned off, when this happens, their profile pic appear instead, and speed is restored.
- When the teacher is to address a sizeable number of students, they are advised to use live stream, rather

than using video meet or better still pre-record and share to them.

- For students with a hearing deficiency, with the live caption, turned on, and their response can be captured and recorded.

January 2020

As of January 2020, some cool features were added to Google Classroom, these include:

Originality report

This feature allows teachers to use originality reports on three assignments in a class. It helps the student improve their writing by flagging missing citations and highlighting some source material. When teachers receive work from the student, a verification process is started to vet its academic integrity and provide real-time feedback using a grading tool.

Rubrics – Already discussed, visit the previous chapter.

June 2019

Redesigned Student Assignment Page

This makes communication between teachers and students better and easier and also for students to submit work.

Gradebook

The Grades Page – It affords teachers the freedom to record and return grades to students, and all this is done on the grade page.

Grading Systems – Different grading systems can now be selected by teachers for each of their classes.

Grade Categories – Grade categories can currently be assigned to classwork posts by teachers.

Overall Grade – Teachers can now allow students from a class to see their overall grades.

Docs Grading Tools – This tool will enable teachers to give students feedback and assign grades.

April 2019

Posts to the Top – All new works are now posted to the top of the Classroom Page

Filter the Classwork Page by Topic – This tool is for teachers, to filter through the classwork page thoroughly.

March 2019

Private Comment Notifications – Private notifications can be received separately from work notifications, and you can either turn it off or on.

January 2019

New Look – An upgrade was done on the designs and theme to be more work-friendly and attractive.

Drag and Drop Classwork – Topics and personal posts can be organized easily on the classwork page.

Sharing Class Code – This can be shared quickly, as it can be founds at the top of every class stream page.

Conclusion

Distance learning has come a long way over the years, with the sole purpose of bringing education to your doorstep, giving anyone who has the basic knowledge of the internet access to the best of education, available anywhere in the world. Before this innovation, it is usual for you to either quit or pause your current engagement to get a new degree, but you can be engaged and still get a degree and a good one at that. So, distance learning has been much of a blessing. The concept and idea of distance learning will not work, unless there are tools to facilitate it, tools such as: Google Classroom, Apple Classroom etc. Hence this book was written to enlighten and show you the path to follow in creating your own Virtual Classroom, but our focus is the Google Classroom.

Everything you need to know about the Google Classroom, has been revealed in detail, but it is not without flaws and concerns. One such concern being security, and this is an issue with any online program since cybercriminals are always in search of data. The data of students and teachers or users of Google Classroom, have been taken with top priority, as they keep upgrading their system every month, not only to provide you with the best of experience but to provide you with top-notch security of your data. This book reveals all the steps you need to take, and also the full benefits each feature provides, to give you the best virtual learning experience through Google Classroom.

If you have never used a computer before, or you have not attempted any online class before, no problem, in front of you lies the key to your amazing online learning experience. This book also equips teachers with all they require to manage a Google Classroom, and even guardians are not left.

Made in the USA
San Bernardino, CA
19 July 2020

75757959R00058